little & LARGE
sticker activity book

BUGS

Miles Kelly
PUBLISHING

First published in 2003 by Miles Kelly Publishing Ltd
Bardfield Centre, Great Bardfield, Essex, CM7 4SL

Copyright © Miles Kelly Publishing 2003

This edition printed in 2008

2 4 6 8 10 9 7 5 3

Editorial Director: Belinda Gallagher

Art Director: Jo Brewer

Project Manager: Nicola Sail

Designer: Maya Currell

Reprographics: Stephan Davis, Ian Paulyn

Production Manager: Elizabeth Brunwin

British Library Cataloguing-in-Publication Data
A catalogue record for this book is available from the British Library

ISBN 978-1-84236-305-8

Printed in China

All photographs and artworks are from MKP archives

www.mileskelly.net
info@mileskelly.net

www.factsforprojects.com

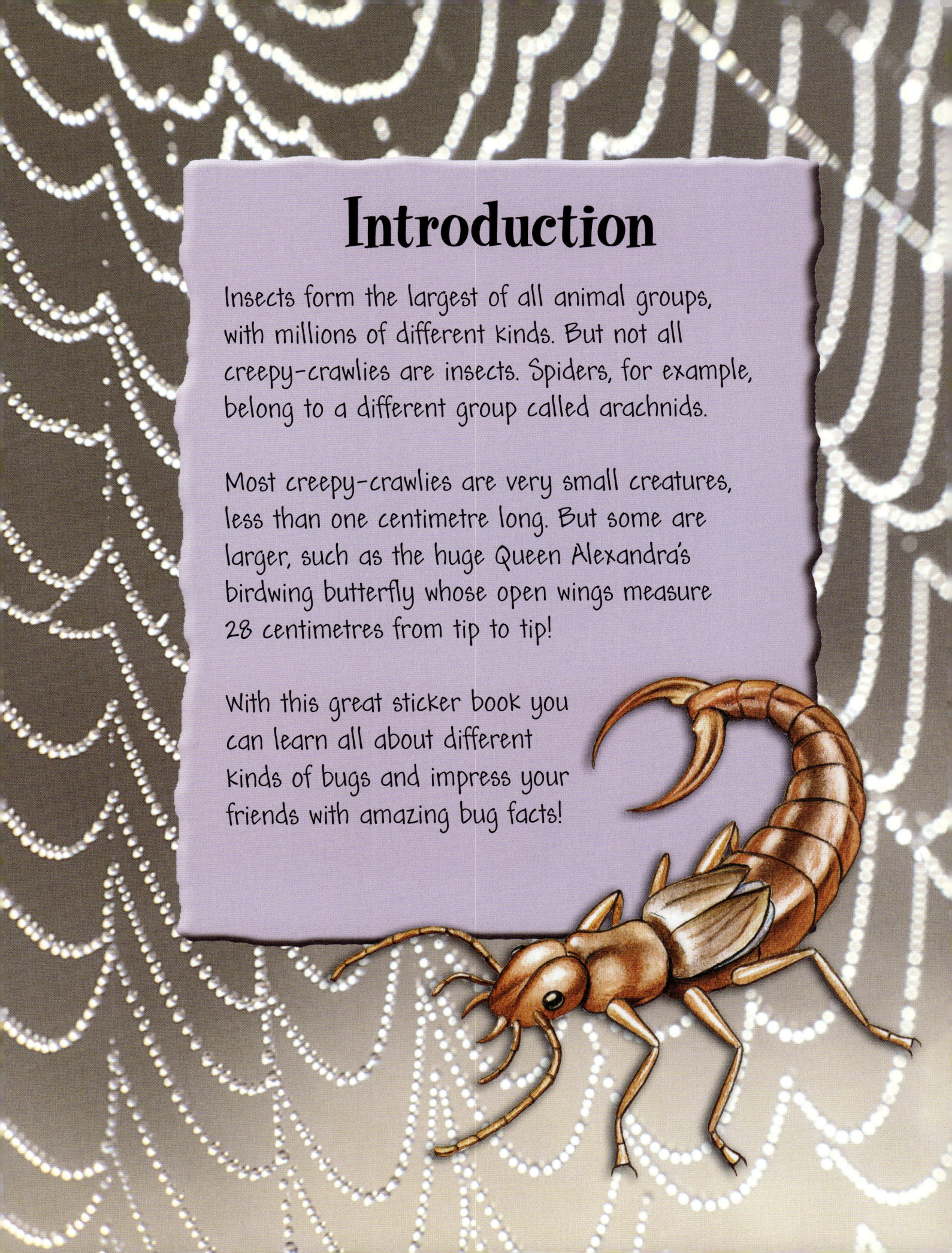

Introduction

Insects form the largest of all animal groups, with millions of different kinds. But not all creepy-crawlies are insects. Spiders, for example, belong to a different group called arachnids.

Most creepy-crawlies are very small creatures, less than one centimetre long. But some are larger, such as the huge Queen Alexandra's birdwing butterfly whose open wings measure 28 centimetres from tip to tip!

With this great sticker book you can learn all about different kinds of bugs and impress your friends with amazing bug facts!

Mini stickers!

 Is the deadly scorpion a beetle or an arachnid? What about a mosquito – is it a type of fly or a member of the butterfly/moth family? Use your mini stickers to see which family some of the world's creepy-crawlies belong to!

Bugs – have two pairs of wings and a beaklike mouth that can pierce and suck

Flies – have a single pair of wings and often carry germs that spread diseases

Arachnids – have a body divided into two sections, eight legs and no wings

Beetles – have toughened front wings that fold over their back wings like a case

Bees/Wasps/Ants – most have two pairs of wings, a narrow waist and females have an ovipositor, or egg-laying organ, at their rear end, that may be used to sting

Crickets/Mantids – most crickets can fly but usually use their strong back legs to escape danger. Mantids are easily recognized by their triangular-shaped head and large eyes

Butterflies/Moths – generally, butterflies are brightly coloured and fly during the day and moths are dull coloured and fly at night

Bugs

▲ Cicada   ▲ Shield bug   ▲ Thorn bug

Flies

▲ Housefly   ▲ Mosquito

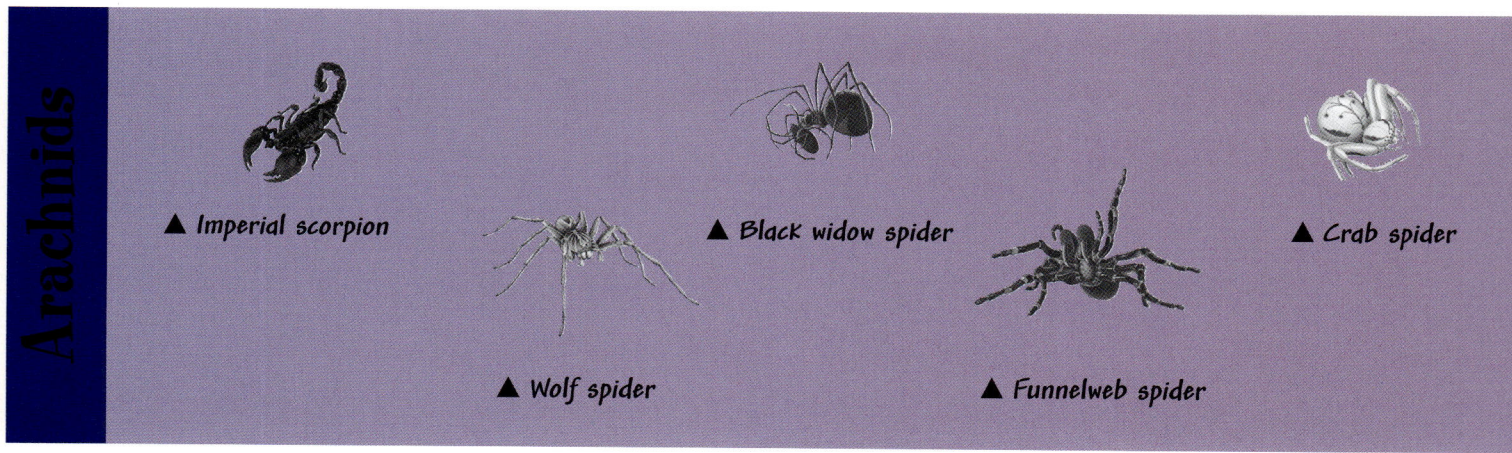

Arachnids

▲ Imperial scorpion   ▲ Black widow spider   ▲ Crab spider

▲ Wolf spider   ▲ Funnelweb spider

Beetles

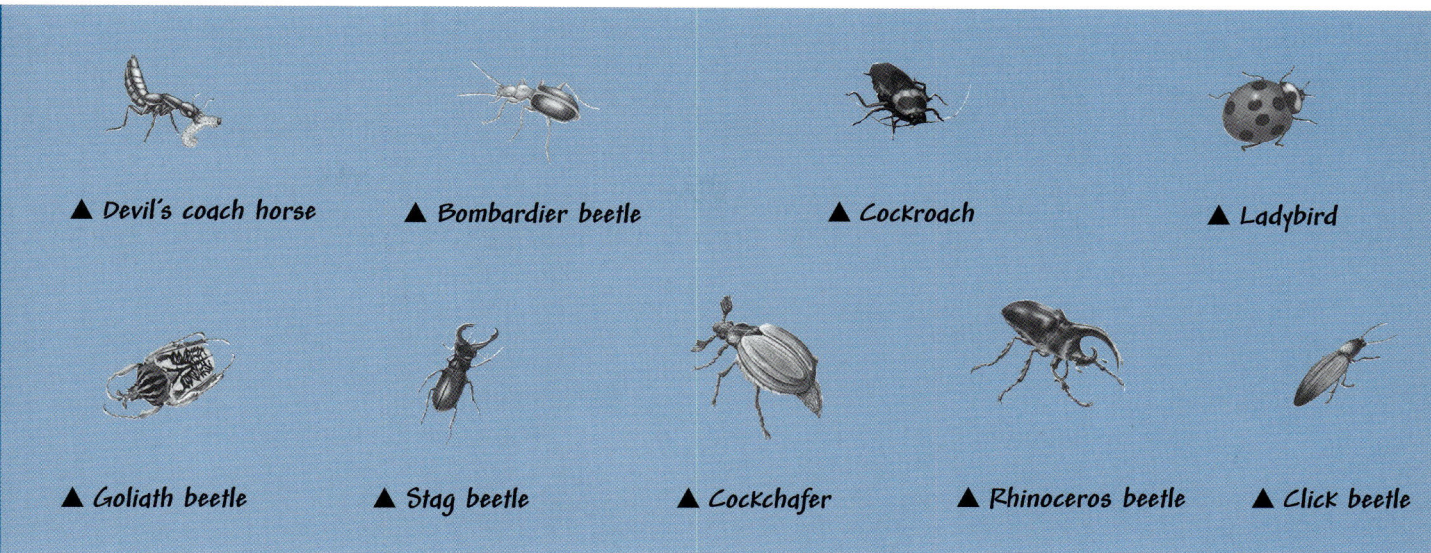

▲ Devil's coach horse ▲ Bombardier beetle ▲ Cockroach ▲ Ladybird

▲ Goliath beetle ▲ Stag beetle ▲ Cockchafer ▲ Rhinoceros beetle ▲ Click beetle

Bees/Wasps/Ants

▲ Leafcutter ants

▲ Hornet ▲ Honey bee

Crickets/Mantids

▲ Locust

▲ Praying mantis ▲ Cricket

Butterflies/Moths

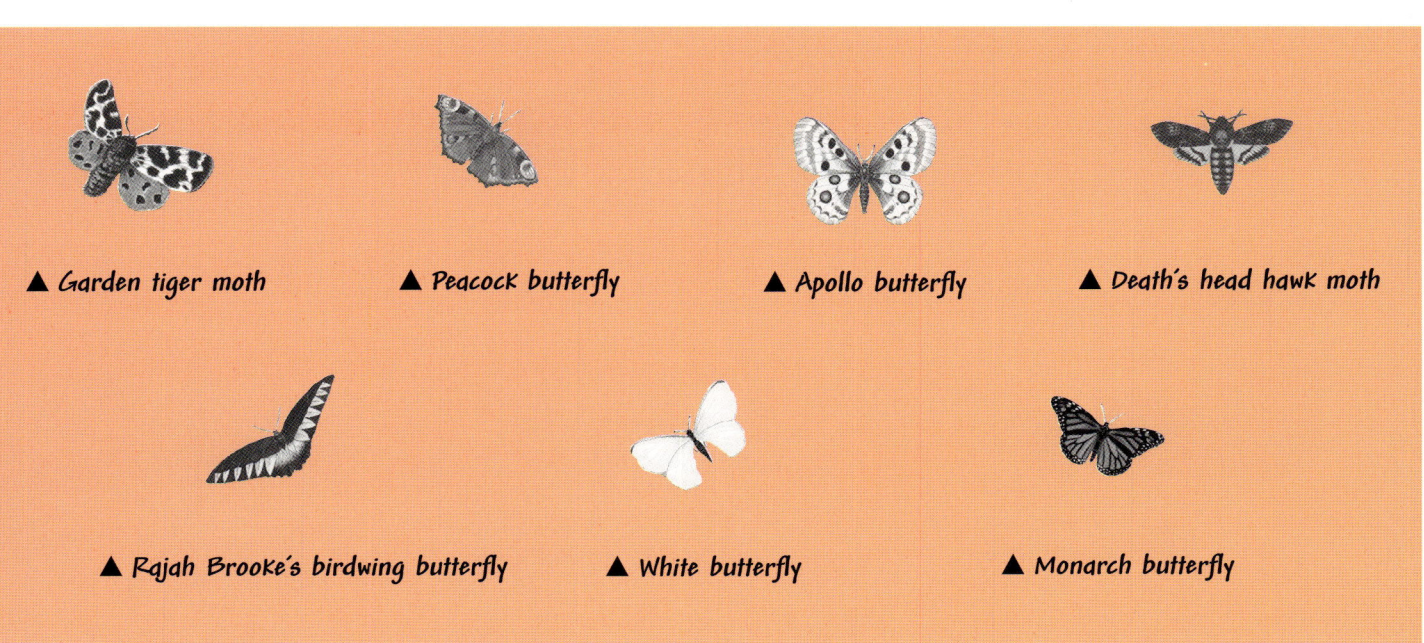

▲ Garden tiger moth ▲ Peacock butterfly ▲ Apollo butterfly ▲ Death's head hawk moth

▲ Rajah Brooke's birdwing butterfly ▲ White butterfly ▲ Monarch butterfly

Creepy-crawlies

◄ Stag beetle
Female's bite is more powerful than the male's, although the male is larger

▲ Mosquito
Among the world's most dangerous pests, spreading diseases such as malaria

▼ Wolf spider
Does not weave webs but chases after victims, like a tiny version of a real wolf

▲ Ladybird
Protects garden plants by eating huge numbers of hungry caterpillars and aphids (greenfly)

► White butterfly
Its young, known as caterpillars, eat the leaves of flowers and vegetables

◄ Cicada
Makes a buzzing noise that can be heard from one kilometre away

▼ Peacock butterfly
Has large spots on its wings that look like the eye spots on peacock feathers

► Housefly
Has tiny taste buds on its feet to sense if where it lands is worth exploring for food

KEY:

 Bugs

 Flies

Arachnids

 Beetles

 Bees/Wasps/Ants

 Crickets/Mantids

 Butterflies/Moths

◄ Click beetle
Can flick itself about 25 centimetres into the air making a click sound

▼ Cricket
Some types can jump more than 3 metres

▼ Rajah Brooke's birdwing butterfly
One of the world's largest butterflies, the birdwing family is now protected by law

▲ Bombardier beetle
Sprays a jet of hot, stinging liquid at attackers

▼ Cockroach
Have low, flat bodies so they can squeeze through tight places in search of food

► Locust
Groups of these can eat massive areas of crops leaving people to starve

▼ Black widow spider
Has a poisonous bite that is strong enough to kill a human

◄ Devil's coach horse
Member of a group of beetles that walks huge distances to find food

For its size, a green tiger beetle runs ten times as fast as a person! It runs at about 60-70 centimetres a second. That is like a human sprinter running 100 metres in one second!

Tarantula!

The biggest spiders in the world are hairy and huge – bigger than your hand! Tarantulas are also known as bird-eating spiders as they really do eat birds, especially baby birds in nests.

These large spiders live in warm, tropical places. Most are not poisonous and rely on their strength and size to catch prey.

▲ This female tarantula is guarding her eggs, which are surrounded by a shell, or cocoon, of silk. When the babies hatch, they will look like tiny versions of their mother.

Make a wool web

You will need:
• white wool • twigs or pipe cleaners • black paper

1. Weave white wool around a star-shaped construction of twigs or pipe cleaners.
2. Cut out a black paper spider and hide it in the web.
3. Hang up the spider's web and see what you can catch!

▲ Housefly

▲ Peacock butterfly

▲ Cicada

▲ Wolf spider

▲ White butterfly

▲ Ladybird

▲ Stag beetle

▲ Mosquito

Creepy-crawlies

▼ Housefly

▶ Peacock butterfly

▼ Cicada

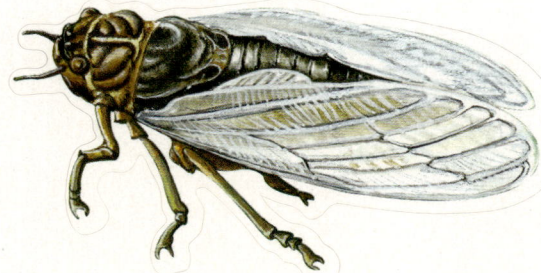

▼ Wolf spider

▶ Ladybird

▲ White butterfly

◀ Stag beetle

▲ Mosquito

▲ Devil's coach horse

▲ Bombardier beetle

▲ Black widow spider

▲ Cricket

▲ Locust

▲ Cockroach

▲ Click beetle

▲ Rajah Brooke's birdwing butterfly

Creepy-crawlies

▼ Devil's coach horse

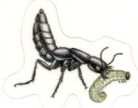

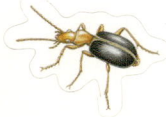

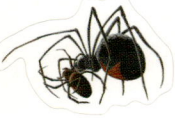

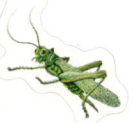

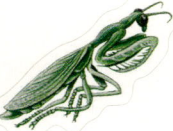

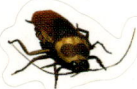

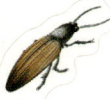

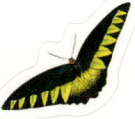

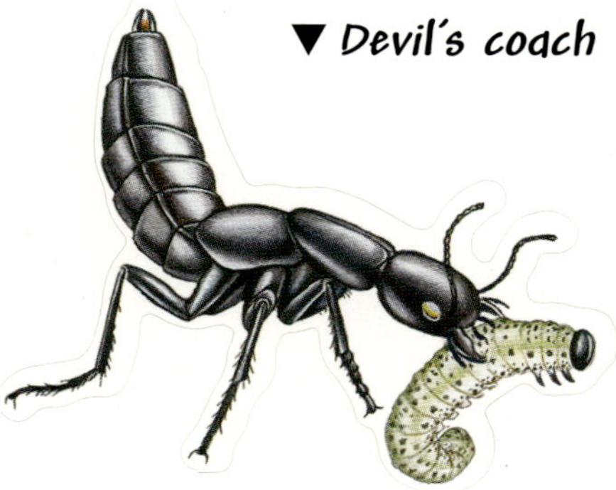

▼ Bombardier beetle

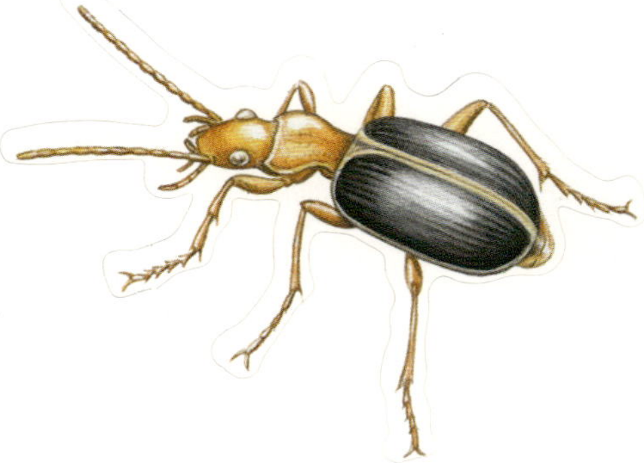

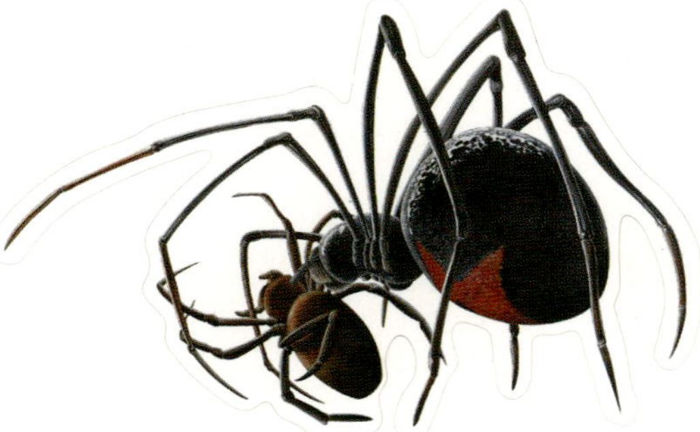

◀ Black widow spider

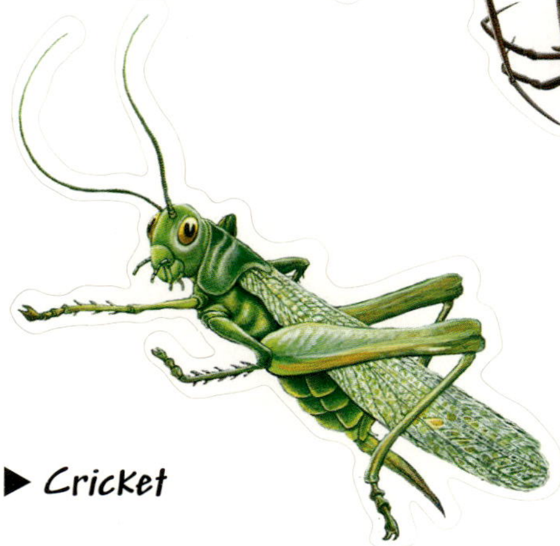

▶ Cricket

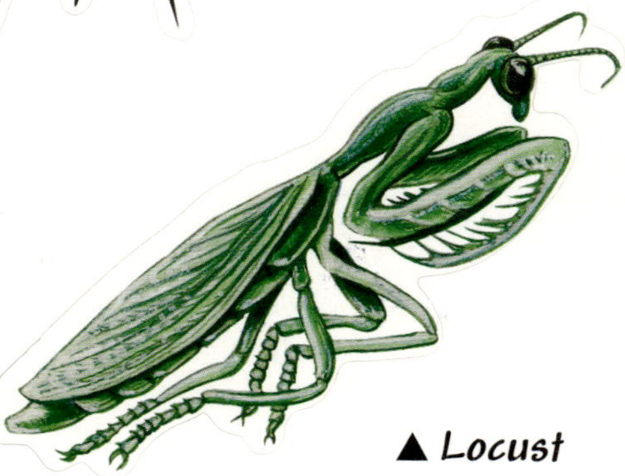

▲ Locust

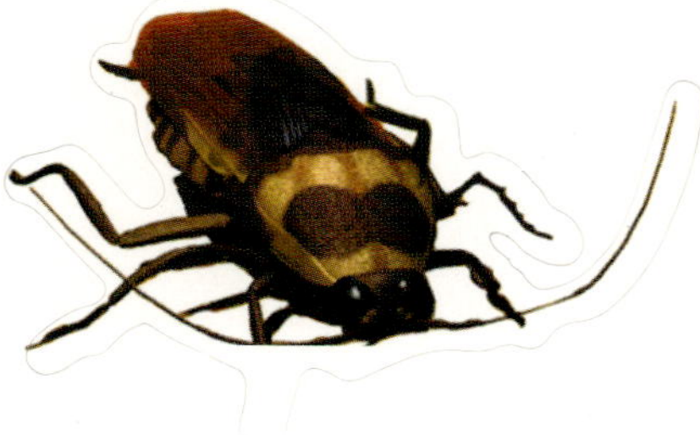

◀ Cockroach

▲ Click beetle

▶ Rajah Brooke's birdwing butterfly

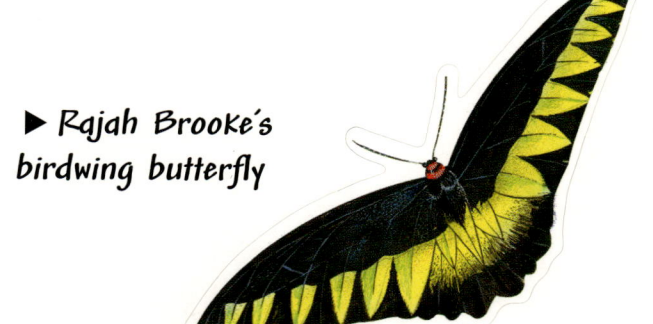

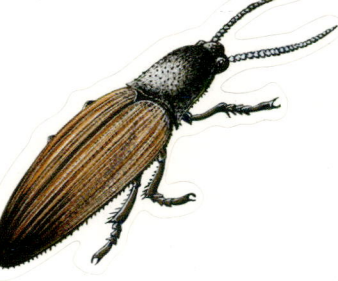

▼ Garden tiger moth

▲ Funnelweb spider

◀ Shield bug

◀ Hornet

▶ Honey bee

▲ Cockchafer

◀ Praying mantis

▶ Thorn bug

▲ Funnelweb spider

▲ Garden tiger moth

▲ Shield bug

▲ Hornet

▲ Cockchafer

▲ Honey bee

▲ Praying mantis

▲ Thorn bug

Creepy-crawlies

▼ Leafcutter ants

▶ Imperial scorpion

▼ Death's head hawk moth

▼ Crab spider

▼ Monarch butterfly

◀ Rhinoceros beetle

▼ Apollo butterfly

▲ Goliath beetle

▲ Leafcutter ants

▲ Imperial scorpion

▲ Death's head hawk moth

▲ Crab spider

▲ Monarch butterfly

▲ Rhinoceros beetle

▲ Apollo butterfly

▲ Goliath beetle

Long-distance fliers

Monarch butterflies fly farther than any other insect. Each year these huge butterflies travel hundreds of kilometres on long journeys, called migrations.

After a winter rest in southern North America, monarchs set off north in spring. They stop on the journey to breed, then die. Their offspring continue the journey. This cycle is repeated when the butterflies return in the autumn.

The bright patterns and spots on a monarch's body warn enemies that this butterfly tastes horrible

Creepy-crawlies

 ◄ **Praying mantis**
Its name comes from the fact that its front legs are folded, like a person with hands together in prayer

Honey bee ▼
Provides honey and wax, and pollinates most of the world's plants

▲ **Thorn bug**
Sits on a twig pretending to be a real thorn

▼ **Hornet**
A large type of wasp with a jagged sting on its rear end

▼ **Shield bug**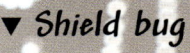
Broad, flat bodies are shaped like the shield carried by a medieval knight-in-armour

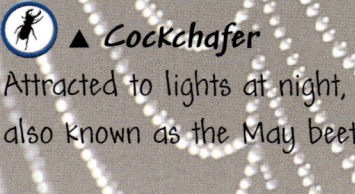

▲ **Cockchafer**
Attracted to lights at night, also known as the May beetle

◄ **Garden tiger moth**
Its bright markings warn predators to keep away as it is not very tasty

▼ **Funnelweb spider**
Makes a funnel-shaped web that leads into its lair – under a rock or root

KEY:

 Bugs   Flies   Arachnids  Beetles  Bees/Wasps/Ants  Crickets/Mantids  Butterflies/Moths

▼ Goliath beetle
World's heaviest beetle from tropical Africa

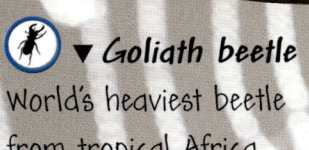

► Apollo butterfly
Body is covered with fur to protect it from the cold in its mountain home

◄ Rhinoceros beetle
Can carry 850 times its own weight, making it 50 times stronger than you

▲ Monarch butterfly
May fly 150 kilometres a day when migrating

► Death's head hawk moth
Has a pattern on its back that looks like a human skull

► Crab spider
Name comes from the fact that they walk sideways like a real crab

► Imperial scorpion
Often hunt after dark catching prey by touch

◄ Leafcutter ants
Harvest leaves that they use at their nest to grow fungi, which they eat

Many kinds of insect find animal droppings delicious. Various types of beetle lay their eggs in droppings, then the larvae hatch out and eat the dung!

The biggest and best!

A web-spinning spider makes a new web almost every night – it eats the old one to recycle (use again) the silk threads.

There are over one million kinds of insect – more than any other kind of animal. And scientists are still discovering new ones!

A single bee would have to visit more than 4000 flowers to make a tablespoon of honey.

Read on to find out about some of the record-breaking bugs

• The African Goliath beetle is the world's heaviest insect. It weighs about 100 kilograms and at 11 centimetres long is almost as big as an adult person's hand!

• The fastest fliers in the insect world include dragonflies, which can reach speeds of up to 58 kilometres an hour.

• The Australian redback spider is one of the most deadly of a group called widow spiders. These spiders get their name because, once they have mated, the female may well eat the male!

Q: What is the biggest moth in the world?
A: A mammoth!

Life of a butterfly

Discover more about a butterfly's life

▲ 1. The butterfly lays its egg

◀ 2. Caterpillar hatches

▶ 3. When fully grown the caterpillar is ready to turn into a pupa

▶ 4. The adult butterfly pushes its way out of the pupa

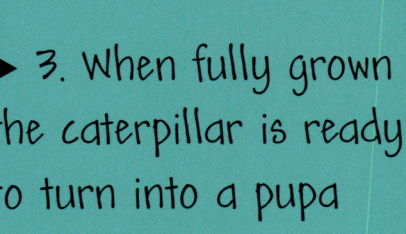

◀ 5. The butterfly spreads and dries its wings and flies away

No other insect flies like the butterfly. It flaps its wings like a bird.

Certain kinds of termite eat away at wood until it is almost hollow. It then collapses into a pile of dust if anyone touches it!

Courtship is a dangerous time for the praying mantis. The female is much bigger than the male and as soon as they have mated, she may eat him!

Q: Where would you put an injured insect?
A: In an antbulance!

Bug facts

🐛 Mosquitos are bloodsuckers – they stick a needle-like tube into the skin and suck up a tiny amount of blood.

🐛 Fleas are the champion leaping insects for their size. At only 2–3 millimetres long, they can leap more than 100 times their body size – over 30 centimetres.

🐛 Most spiders and other arachnids have eight eyes, but they still don't see very well.

Test your memory!

How much can you remember from your bugs sticker activity book? Find out below!

1. Which is larger – the male or female stag beetle?
2. Does the wolf spider weave webs or chase its prey?
3. From how far away can the cicada's buzzing noise be heard?
4. Which insect can spread malaria?
5. How high can a click beetle flick itself into the air?
6. Which beetle sprays a jet of hot stinging liquid at attackers?
7. Which bug can eat lots of crops leaving people to starve?
8. Which are the biggest spiders in the world?
9. How fast does a tiger beetle run?
10. Which is the world's heaviest insect?

Q: What do you call an ant in space?
A: An astronant!

11. How many times its own weight can a rhinoceros beetle carry?

12. Which insects fly the farthest?

13. When migrating, how many kilometres a day might a monarch butterfly travel?

14. A butterfly flies in the same way as which other animal?

15. Which are the champion leaping insects for their size?

16. How many eyes do arachnids have?

17. What is it known as when scorpions lift their bodies off the ground to cool down?

18. Is a cicada an insect or an arachnid?

19. Which type of insect pollinates most of the world's plants?

20. Which insect has a pattern on its back that looks like a human skull?

Answers:

1. The male 2. Chase its prey 3. One kilometre 4. A mosquito 5. 25 centimetres 6. The bombardier beetle 7. The locust 8. The tarantula or bird-eating spider 9. Up to 60–70 centimetres a second 10. The Goliath beetle 11. 850 times 12. The monarch butterfly 13. 150 kilometres 14. A bird 15. Fleas 16. Eight 17. Stilting 18. Insect 19. Honey bee 20. Death's head hawk moth

● All spiders spin silk, but not all of them make webs. The spitting spider catches prey by spitting a sticky gum over them.

● Hot scorpions sometimes lift their bodies off the ground to let air get underneath to cool them down – this is called stilting.

● The buzzing of a fly is the sound of its wings beating!

Q: What has antlers and sucks blood?
A: A moosequito!

Other sticker books

You can now have even more fun and collect
all the sticker books in this series

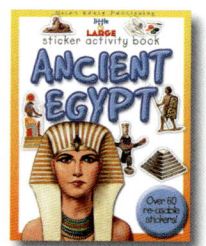

978-1-84236-660-8

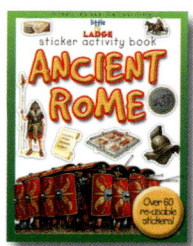

978-1-84236-661-5

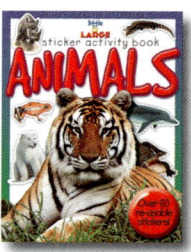

978-1-84236-303-4

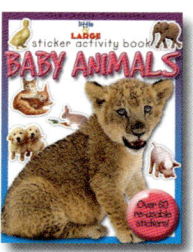

978-1-84236-244-0

978-1-84236-513-7

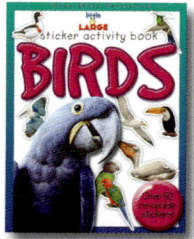

978-1-84236-304-1

978-1-84236-305-8

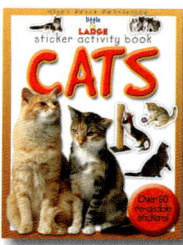

978-1-84236-662-2

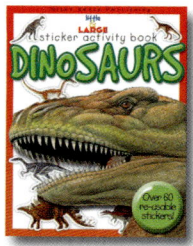

978-1-84236-302-7

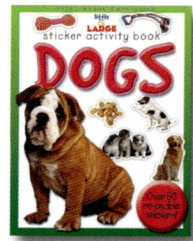

978-1-84236-663-9

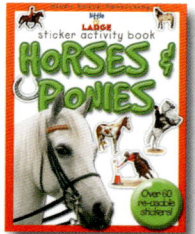

978-1-84236-514-4

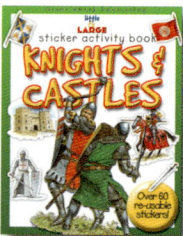

978-1-84236-255-6

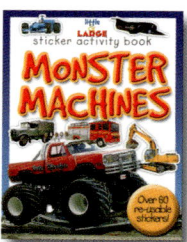

978-1-84236-671-4

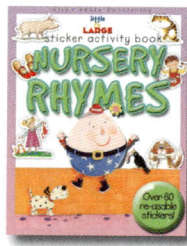

978-1-84236-246-4

978-1-84236-307-2

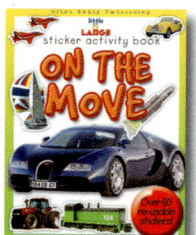

978-1-84236-245-7

978-1-84236-306-5

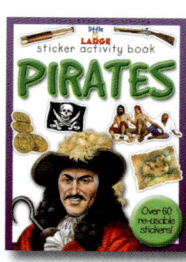

978-1-84236-669-1

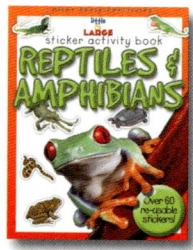

978-1-84236-254-9

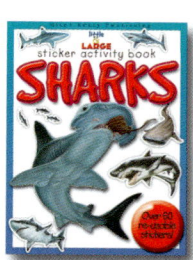

978-1-84236-512-0

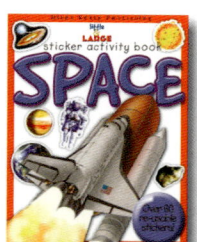

978-1-84236-247-1

978-1-84236-515-1

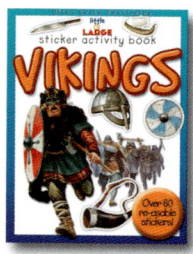

978-1-84236-668-4

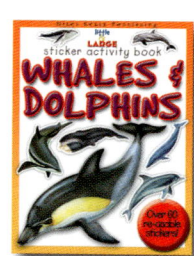

978-1-84236-672-1

978-1-84236-498-7